All About WOLVES

by Meish Goldish

Chapters

Where Are the Wolves?...................2
A Wolf's Life......................................6
Wolves in Our World.....................13

Orlando Boston Dallas Chicago San Diego

Visit *The Learning Site!*
www.harcourtschool.com

Where Are the Wolves?

Have you ever seen a wolf? It is the largest wild member of the dog family. The two main types of wolves are gray wolves and red wolves.

Most wolves are gray wolves. They live mainly in Alaska, China, Canada, and Russia. Some also live in the northern United States.

Red wolves live in a few places in the southern United States. They are smaller than gray wolves in size and in number. Today, only a few hundred red wolves exist.

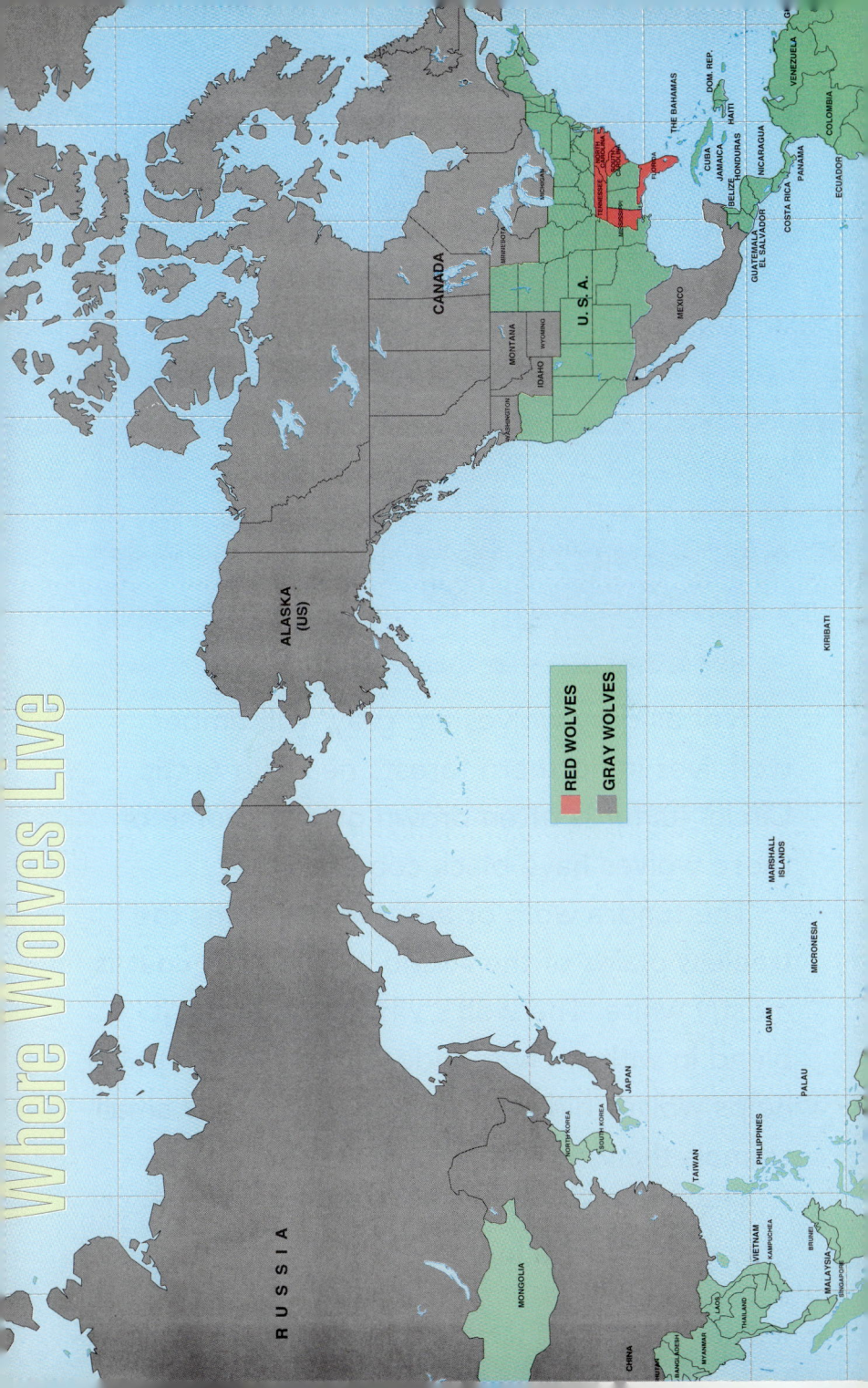

Not all gray wolves are gray. The timber wolf lives in northern forests near the Arctic Circle. Its fur is often brown or gray. Some of these wolves have black coats.

The tundra wolf, or arctic wolf, roams the treeless plains of the Arctic. Its thick fur coat is mostly white. The wolf's white coat helps it blend in with snow to hide from hunters. It also helps wolves hide from rabbits and other small animals the wolves are hunting.

The Mexican wolf is the smallest kind of gray wolf. People in Mexico call it *el lobo*.

A wolf looks similar to a German shepherd dog. However, a wolf has longer legs, bigger feet, and a wider head. It also has a big, furry tail.

From its nose to the tip of its tail, an adult male wolf can be between 5 and $6\frac{1}{2}$ feet long. It stands about $2\frac{1}{2}$ feet high at the shoulders. The female is smaller than the male.

A fully grown gray wolf usually weighs from 75 to 120 pounds. However, a wolf weighing 175 pounds was once caught.

A Wolf's Life

The mating season for wolves is between January and April. During that time, the parents prepare a den in a cave or other hidden spot. The female gives birth after about 9 weeks.

A female wolf usually has about 5 or 6 babies at a time. Baby wolves are called pups. At birth, a pup is about 8 inches long and weighs about 1 pound. It is a tender creature that cannot see or hear at first. It completely depends on its mother for food and warmth.

For the first 2 or 3 weeks, baby wolves live only on their mothers' milk. Then they start to eat meat. Their parents find the meat and bring it to them. The parents also take the pups out of the den for short trips.

Outside the den, pairs of pups play to see which can stand over the other one. Their play gets rougher until one pup gives up and rolls over. In this way, the pups start to learn who will be strongest and who will be weakest in the group.

After about 2 months, the pups leave the den for good. They live in an area that is not hidden, as the den was. The pups stay there during the summer. The parents continue to bring them food. In the fall, the parents begin to teach them how to live in the wild.

Wolves travel and hunt in groups called packs. Some wolves stay in the same pack their whole lives, but others do not. A young wolf may leave the pack by the age of 2. The lone wolf travels by itself until it finds a partner. Then the partners mate to start their own pack.

The wolves that hunt together in a pack are delighted with each other's company. Most packs have about 8 members.

The wolves in a pack are not all equal, however. When a stronger wolf meets a weaker wolf, they behave in certain ways. The stronger wolf stands straight with its tail and ears up. It may growl and show its sharp teeth. The weaker wolf lowers its head and ears. It puts its tail between its legs. Sometimes it whines or whimpers to show that it knows the stronger wolf is the boss.

Wolves are cunning hunters. Pack members work together to catch their prey. Hunting often begins around dusk, when the sun goes down. First, pack members gather to howl loudly. The noise warns other wolf packs to stay out of the area. Then the hunt starts.

The pack travels together until they find their prey. Wolves often go after large animals such as deer and moose. They also hunt rabbits, beavers, and mice.

Often, a wolf pack will follow a herd of deer. The wolves move in a single line at first. Slowly, they pick up speed and sneak closer to their prey. They are careful to move quietly. The snap of a brittle twig could warn the herd that danger is near. Finally, the wolf pack rushes after the herd.

As the herd runs away, many animals are too fast for the wolves. Others protect themselves by kicking or using their horns. So, the wolves look for the member that is slowest or weakest.

A hunt may last several hours before the prey is finally brought down. Sometimes, entire days or weeks pass before a wolf pack finally catches an animal. A wolf can go about two weeks without any food.

By killing the weakest animals, wolves actually help the natural world. The strongest animals produce strong, healthy babies. Also, animal herds have more food for themselves without their weak or sick members.

Wolves in Our World

Long ago, wolves roamed free in many parts of the world. People didn't mind, because wolves avoid humans as much as possible.

Native Americans admired how the wolves worked together in packs. Many Indians even named themselves after wolves.

Over time, however, other people grew afraid of wolves. They no longer embraced wolves as harmless neighbors. Eventually, they told stories like "The Three Little Pigs," in which the wolf was mean and dangerous.

What made people turn against wolves? Mostly, it was because of food.

During the 1800s, settlers moved across America. They raised sheep and cattle on land where wolves roamed.

The wolves attacked the farm animals. Farmers would latch their gates, but the attacks continued. As a result, farmers began to hunt down the wolves. By 1930, hardly any wolves were alive in the United States.

In 1973, the U.S. government passed a law to protect animals in danger of dying out. Hunters were not allowed to kill wolves anywhere in the United States except Alaska.

Because of the law, the number of wolves in America has grown. About 1,000 gray wolves now live in Minnesota. Gray wolves also roam the wild in Wyoming and Idaho. Some red wolves roam the wild in North Carolina and Tennessee.

Many people today still fear wolves. They think that wolves attack humans. In fact, wolves do not attack people. They are shy animals that try to stay away from humans.

No one knows for sure what the future holds for wolves. In the United States, they are still protected as endangered animals. Since wolves are protected, they will keep growing in number. They will continue to bring beauty and strength to the world.